MALCOLM L. REID

PREHISTORIC HOUSES
IN BRITAIN

SHIRE ARCHAEOLOGY

Cover illustration
Reconstruction of an iron age crannog in a Scottish loch, by Frank Gardiner.

British Library Cataloguing in Publication Data:
Reid, M. L. Prehistoric Houses in Britain. — (Shire Archaeology Series; No. 70).
I. Title II. Series 936.1
ISBN 0-7478-0218-1.

This book is dedicated to my wife Gill, who has been a constant help throughout all stages of my research, and to Professor Richard Bradley, whose enthusiasm has brought prehistory to life.

Published by
SHIRE PUBLICATIONS LTD
Cromwell House, Church Street, Princes Risborough,
Buckinghamshire HP27 9AJ, UK.

Series Editor: James Dyer.

ISBN 0 7478 0218 1.

First published 1993.

Printed in Great Britain by
CIT Printing Services, Press Buildings,
Merlins Bridge, Haverfordwest, Dyfed SA61 1XF.

Contents

Acknowledgements

I am extremely grateful to Frank Gardiner for his illustrations, which have provided an added insight into the building techniques of our prehistoric ancestors, also for his help and advice, and for making the production of this book so pleasurable. I am indebted to Professor Barry Cunliffe for permission to reproduce a photograph (figure 36 in this publication); also to Dr Nicholas Dixon, Daryll Garton and Dr Harold Mytum for information on the excavations they have conducted, and to Dr Michael Parker Pearson for a theoretical paper prior to publication. John Barrett, Professor Richard Bradley, James Dyer, Jacqueline Fearn and Professor Michael Fulford have kindly commented on the draft text.

List of illustrations

1
Introduction

Shelter is one of the essentials for sustaining human life. Besides being places of refuge and protection from the elements, dwellings fulfil a range of basic needs: for warmth, a place to cook, eat and sleep. A dwelling is therefore a most intimate expression of the occupants' values and needs.

Archaeologists and architectural historians have traditionally viewed prehistoric dwellings as primitive and crude. Commonly referred to as 'huts', these structures were presumed to have been erected by people with little skill or technical knowledge. However, if seen in relation to the development of technology, it would appear that the majority of prehistoric dwellings were skilfully constructed. Many also seem to have been carefully designed, not only to fulfil basic domestic requirements, but according to the social customs and rituals of everyday life.

The purpose of this book is to demonstrate the range of house types and styles in prehistoric Britain, from the late mesolithic to the Roman period, and to offer some explanations for the differences in building design. It will concentrate on those structures that were of a reasonably permanent construction.

Most, if not all, houses in prehistoric Britain were probably designed and built by those who lived in them. Within each community there are likely to have been individuals who were particularly skilled in building construction, techniques having been passed down from one generation to another. In this way the apparent diversity of building types became established, corresponding to some extent to different tribal or ethnic groups. Similarities which occur in the design of prehistoric houses in the different parts of Britain may relate not only to the solving of structural problems but also to the comparable nature of domestic life and social organisation.

Before looking at particular examples of prehistoric dwellings, consideration will be given to the methods and materials used in construction, the factors that have affected their preservation, and how the excavation of prehistoric houses has advanced since the late nineteenth century.

All dates quoted in this book are in calendar years. The mesolithic/neolithic transition took place about 4300 BC and marks the change from a principally nomadic way of life, centred around hunting and foraging for food, to a more settled existence, with farming as the principal means of food production. This change also brought about the development of new tool types. Towards the end of the neolithic, around 2500 BC, objects made of copper were introduced into Britain. By 2100 BC copper had given way to bronze production — the bronze age. This period was in turn followed by the iron age, which started around 700 BC and marks the change to the manufacture of iron tools. Following the Roman conquest of Britain in the first century AD, the northern and western regions of the country remained largely outside the area of Roman domination, with little integration and adoption of Roman ways of life, including the building of villa-farms. In these areas many native communities continued to construct their homes according to traditional methods.

2
Materials and the surviving evidence

Most prehistoric houses in Britain do not survive to any appreciable height; indeed for most only their foundations remain. The different states of preservation of these buildings depend to a large extent on the materials available and chosen for construction. Survival may be enhanced by the formation of subsequent deposits, burying the remains, whereas later activities on the site, such as excavation or cultivation, can often lead to the destruction of earlier structures and related deposits.

Building materials

The materials used to construct houses during the prehistoric period tended to be those that were locally and freely available. The walls of prehistoric houses were built of stone or of timber-framed construction. (Timber framing is used here to refer to buildings that have a framed superstructure, whether of post or of stake construction.) Turf was also used but, as it is not particularly strong or durable on its own, it was often stacked next to a timber frame or placed on top of a stone foundation to give a wall additional height.

In those areas where stone has traditionally been used as a building material a basic division can be seen between the south and east of Britain and the rest of the country to the west and north (figure 1). It is clear that these areas are a reflection of the topography and underlying geology and are often referred to as the highland and lowland zones. In the highland zone during the prehistoric period many houses were built of stone (that is to say that their walls were constructed of stone), although in various areas at various times timber was used in preference to the stone of good or reasonable quality that was to be found near at hand. In these situations it might be suspected that the people did not have the technical skill to construct in stone. But this was often not so, as there were many later prehistoric settlements of timber houses which were enclosed by defences including skilfully constructed stone revetments. It is impossible to say why such choices were made. They may for example be in response to practical or material considerations or relate to traditional practices.

Throughout the prehistoric period it would appear that stone for building was not quarried on a large scale. Much came from accessible outcrops and loose material lying on the surface or embedded in the subsoil. The best stone for building is that which is reasonably hard and does not weather easily but which can be split into slabs or blocks without too much difficulty. Large angular boulders were often used,

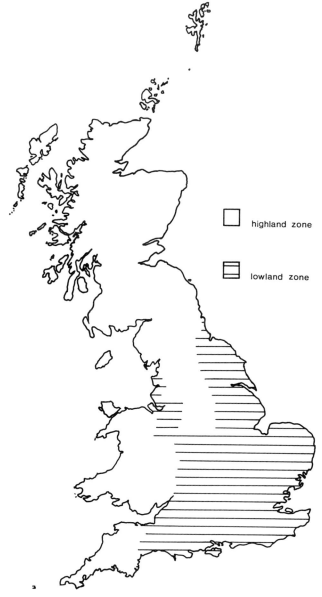

1. Map showing the highland and lowland regions of Britain. In the highland zone stone is often available and has commonly been used for construction.

with the gaps being filled in with smaller stones. The majority of stone-built structures in the prehistoric period in Britain were of drystone construction; clay was occasionally used as a base for stonework or as bonding material. The rock types found in the north and west of Scotland, most notably the beds of Old Red Sandstone, enabled the prehistoric communities in these areas eventually to build houses of monumental proportions.

Beginning about 6800 years ago, many of the natural woods and forests which were once so extensive and characteristic of the uplands of Britain were cleared in successive periods so that land could be farmed, as well as to provide fuel and timber for construction. Analysis of fossil pollen grains preserved in peat and other deposits laid down in prehistoric times has revealed that in Scotland the Northern and Western Isles and much of the Atlantic coastal areas of the mainland were never heavily wooded. Tree cover in these areas tended to be dominated by birch and hazel. These trees are fast growing and as a consequence are not particularly strong. They tend, therefore, not to be suitable as load-bearing timbers for construction. In those areas of Scotland prehistoric communities were either forced to use the most suitable wood available locally or to bring in timber from further afield, notably from the Caledonian forests, which originally covered much of the Highlands up to 650 metres above sea level. If, as seems likely, timber was acquired from other areas, it probably formed part of an exchange system linking a number of widespread and geographically isolated communities. Driftwood, including timber from North America, is also known to have been used in the construction of prehistoric buildings. There is also some evidence of whalebone having been used for rafters in houses in the Northern and Western Isles.

In the lowland zone the majority of prehistoric houses were of timber-framed construction. This is because there is little stone in this region that was suitable or could be easily quarried by prehistoric communities. For those buildings where load-bearing posts formed the frame it was important that the timber used for this purpose was strong and durable, as well as being relatively easy to work. As oak possesses these qualities, it has been commonly used in many types of construction work, including house building, since prehistory. Where oak was not available, ash, birch, elm and pine would probably have been used for the principal timbers. But all these trees have drawbacks if used for construction: ash is a strong wood but will rot easily when in direct contact with the ground; birch is not very strong and rots easily when in contact with water but if seasoned properly it can be used externally; elm is a tough hard wood, which is resistant to decay as long as it is kept either wet or dry; pine is not a very strong wood but is durable.

An important structural device in the prehistoric period was the wattle hurdle, which could be used to form exterior walls and internal partitions. To ensure a constant supply of wood for hurdlemaking, there must have been some degree of wood management, such as coppicing and pollarding. The principal wood used to make hurdles was hazel, chosen because it is flexible. Birch, ash and willow are also known to have been used for this purpose.

Factors affecting the survival of prehistoric structures

Archaeological sites can be divided into two basic groups: 'dry-land' (the majority), where the subsoil and other deposits below the surface have always been comparatively dry, and 'waterlogged' sites (the

2. The waterlogged remains of structural timbers in the process of excavation at the late bronze age site at Flag Fen, Peterborough, Cambridgeshire.

minority), which have remained consistently wet since their occupation, or where the remains have been subsequently covered by layers of wet impervious clay. Where waterlogged deposits are encountered, including the lower fills of wells, deeply dug pits and ditches on dry-land sites, there is the likelihood of finding a range of well-preserved organic materials, including wooden objects and structural remains. Preservation is due to the anaerobic conditions where oxygen, which normally plays a major part in the decay of such materials, has been excluded. The organic materials which are preserved provide the archaeologist with a fascinating insight into many aspects of everyday life in the past; such material has normally completely disintegrated on most dry-land sites. The most extensive remains of waterlogged prehistoric structures in lowland Britain have been found in the raised mires of the Somerset Levels and in the fens of East Anglia, sealed and surrounded by accumulations of peat. These include complete settlements, wooden trackways and impressive ritual and ceremonial centres (figure 2). Well-preserved remains of timber structures dating from the prehistoric period have also been found in the flood plains of major rivers, sealed under thick deposits of alluvium. In Scotland prehistoric island dwellings known as crannogs have been preserved in estuaries and many freshwater lochs (see cover illustration).

Where waterlogging occurs, parts of the superstructure may survive, but the degree of preservation will ultimately depend on what happened to that structure after it was abandoned; for example, whether it was left to fall down, or whether it was dismantled so that at least some of the timbers could be reused elsewhere. Where internal floors and features such as hearths and storage containers are preserved, these, together with any associated artefacts, enable the archaeologist to suggest how various parts of a building were used.

On most dry-land sites that have been intensively cultivated, all that usually remains of timber houses is the more deeply excavated foundations — holes or trenches — which mark the locations of posts, planking or wattle hurdles. The position, shape and size of former timbers may be indicated by the charred or rotted remains of the stumps, which appear as dark stains in the soil, known to archaeologists as *post-pipes* (figure 3). The truncating action of the plough usually means that all the floor-level deposits, associated artefacts and internal features have been removed, and as a consequence it is extremely difficult to suggest what activities were carried out in a particular building. However, in certain situations intensive cultivation can have a beneficial effect in helping to preserve archaeological remains. In areas of limestone and chalk erosion can lead to the formation of thick soily deposits at the base of dry valleys. Where ploughing takes place, this will often have

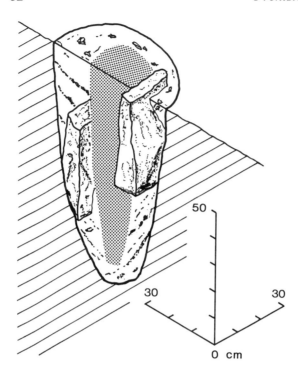

3. Three-dimensional drawing of a half section through a large post hole, showing post-pipe (stippled) and stone packing.

the effect of intensifying the whole process, which is known as *colluviation*. Where prehistoric settlements have been located in the bottoms of these dry valleys, it is likely that the structural remains will be covered over and hence protected against the destructive actions of the plough. The deposits of alluvium within the flood plains of major rivers also offer a similar degree of protection.

Sandy soils near to the coast are often extremely fertile and easily tilled, making them very attractive as areas for settlement, especially in the prehistoric period. The unconsolidated nature of these soils, which makes them particularly susceptible to wind erosion, together with the ravages of the sea, can have the effect of exposing, destroying or quickly burying archaeological remains. The changes affecting coastal areas have led to the discovery of some very well-preserved settlements, perhaps the most famous being the neolithic settlement at Skara Brae, Orkney.

Hillforts and the smaller defended settlements that dominated the landscape of many parts of Britain during much of the first millennium BC may still offer some protection to the buildings within. If cultivation has never taken place within the interior, buildings will often remain in a good state of preservation, some recognisable on the surface as stone foundations or as a series of low, well-defined earthworks, as, for example, in part of the interior of the hillfort at Hod Hill, Dorset. On those sites where occupation lasted for a long period and was particularly intense, there is a tendency for one phase of occupation to seal another, with the result that a whole succession of buildings may be relatively well-preserved, such as those within the hillfort at Danebury, Hampshire.

These defended settlements clearly indicate that the first millennium BC was a time of social tension and unrest. Although the causes of this tension were undoubtedly complicated and various, it is known that they took place against a background of worsening climate — it was becoming cooler and wetter. The expansion of settlement into marginal areas that had taken place during the second millennium tended to stop as thin and poorly drained soils became infertile and the climatic conditions encouraged the formation of blanket peat. As the situation got worse in these upland areas, communities were forced eventually to abandon their homes, moving to more fertile regions, where increasing demands on the land led to a period of aggressive competition. It is in the upland areas, where the land has not been improved, that some of the best-preserved later prehistoric settlements are found, often associated with other contemporary features, such as field systems, funerary and ceremonial monuments, for example at Merrivale on Dartmoor.

3
Construction and reconstruction

By examining the ground plans of prehistoric houses and comparing the structural elements that survive it is possible to build up a picture of how these dwellings might have looked and how they may have been constructed. To enable a fuller reconstruction to be made, archaeologists have paid particular attention to vernacular buildings in other parts of the world and have carried out numerous experiments, trying to reproduce ancient technology and gain a greater understanding of it.

House shape and the principles of construction

In terms of their plan shape, prehistoric houses can be divided into three basic types: rectangular/sub-rectangular, round and oval. Rectangular/sub-rectangular houses are typical of the neolithic, whereas in the bronze and iron ages all forms are to be found, although by this time the most common type was the round-house. Throughout the prehistoric period it was usual for houses to be constructed as separate units, often forming parts of settlement groups. However, some houses have a distinctly 'semi-detached' appearance, for example when they are connected to one another by conjoining walls or by means of shared entrances and passageways. Prehistoric settlements tended to be occupied for many generations. It is therefore not surprising to find that some houses are joined to, and incorporate, earlier structures or are themselves added to at a later date.

Whatever the form of a building, it is essential that stability and a degree of permanence are achieved. First, a solid, usually level base has to be created to secure the foundation, on which the superstructure, consisting of the walls, upper floor or floors and roof, is erected. On sloping ground a level area, often just enough to contain a house, was produced by quarrying into the slope. It is vital that for any building the weight and pressure of the roof and any upper floors are distributed equally and the gravitational forces channelled downward to the foundations by means of load-bearing walls, posts or piers. Any part of the construction which is designed to be load-bearing must be materially strong and well-built and will often require relatively deep foundations. In rectangular and sub-rectangular buildings the long enclosing walls tend to take much of the weight of the roof and upper floors. In circular buildings the pressures exerted by the roof must be carried equally round the structure, otherwise the walls will be pushed outward and the building will collapse. When constructing oval buildings, longitudinal as well as circular forces have to be countered. The overall plan shape of prehistoric houses does not seem to have been influenced in any significant way by the materials available for construction.

Construction methods: wood

Until the production of bronze tools in Britain around 2100 BC, timber was felled and worked using axes and adzes made from flint or stone that could be sharpened and polished. Using these tools, and later their metal counterparts, together with wooden mallets and wedges, wood was split into planks, either radially or tangentially, or made into squared timbers (figure 4). The main structural timbers were often left whole (roundwood). Throughout much of the bronze age in Britain bronze appears to have been a rare and highly prized commodity. Many tools used in woodworking, including chisels, knives and gouges, continued to be manufactured from flint. From the surviving structural evidence the development of woodworking joints can be worked out (figure 5). Mortise and tenon and simple forms of the lap and scarf joints are

4. Diagram showing the difference between (a) radial, (b) split planks and (c) squared timbers.

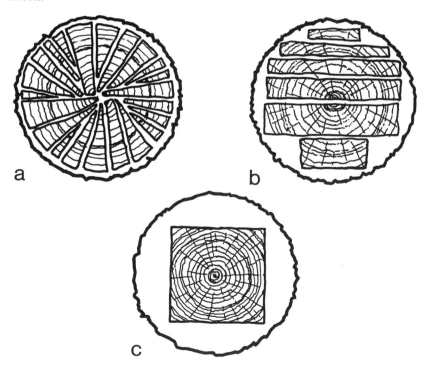

a

b

c

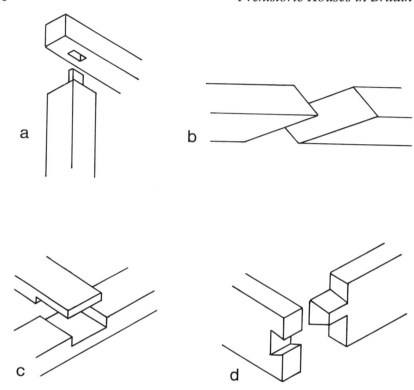

5. Joints used in prehistoric construction: (a) mortise and tenon, (b) scarf, (c) lap, (d) dovetail. (After Hodges.)

known from bronze age contexts, but probably all had developed during the neolithic. Dovetail joints were in use during the iron age. Naturally occurring forked timbers also make good structural supports. Throughout prehistory rope or thong would have been used to lash timbers together, but by the bronze age wooden pegs were also commonly used to secure joints.

By the iron age a virtually full range of woodworking tools had been developed (figure 6), and all were probably in common use throughout Britain. Undoubtedly the most important innovation at this time was the saw, as it allowed more intricate and accurate carpentry to be undertaken. Large iron nails were also used to join major structural timbers together.

It is evident from the remains of prehistoric houses in Britain that since the neolithic a variety of techniques have been employed in the construction of timber-framed walls. Posts and stakes were either hammered into the ground or placed in excavated holes or narrow trenches. The foundation trenches used in the construction of some round-houses are commonly referred to as *ring-grooves*. Sometimes within the holes or trenches stones were tightly packed around the posts to keep them firmly in position. Alternatively, a low stone bank or wall was built next to or around the wooden framework for additional support. The outer wall of many of the more substantial buildings consisted of a series of evenly spaced posts between which were set smaller posts, planks or wattle hurdles. The hurdles were covered with daub or backed with turf. The framework forming the exterior wall of many bronze and iron age round-houses was composed entirely of wattle. Experimental work has shown that, if tightly woven, wattle walls have considerable strength. During the iron age some buildings were founded on sill beams, set in trenches or placed directly on the ground. All that may indicate the position of the latter type are stone spreads that provided the basis for floors, such as those found in the late iron age levels within the hillfort at Moel y Gaer, Clwyd.

The majority of timber-framed houses of neolithic date appear to be rectangular or sub-rectangular in plan. The smallest buildings tend to be single units, with no major internal partitions. Larger houses were divided into a number of bays or rooms. Reconstructing the superstructure of these buildings is especially problematical. In relation to the tools available it seems unlikely that the more technically advanced methods of roof framing — such as the post and truss (figure 7a) — had been developed by this date. The roofs of many such buildings were probably supported by a series of individual uprights connected by mortises and tenons and secured with rope or thongs (figure 7b).

Thatch was probably the most common roofing material, but turf, shingles and animal hides may also have been used. Where thatch was chosen, it would have been important that the roof pitch was at least 45 degrees, to allow surface water to be effectively shed. At the apex of the roof a ridge pole would have been required to support the ends of the rafters. The other ends of the rafters would have been connected to the wall plate, which formed the top part of the wall frame and spread the load of the roof equally round the building. Additional support for the roof was provided by the posts which formed the internal partitions. It seems probable that both hipped and gabled roofs were constructed at this time. The wattle walls of stake-built houses may have been continued up to form a curved roof, in much the same way as the 'beehive' type of round-house.

Using ethnographic analogies, the superstructures of prehistoric timber-framed round-houses probably fall into two basic groups: those where there is no distinction between the enclosing walls and the roof

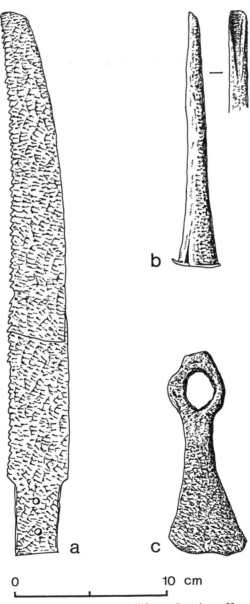

6. Iron woodworking tools from the iron age hillfort at Danebury, Hampshire: (a) saw, (b) gouge, (c) adze. (After Cunliffe.)

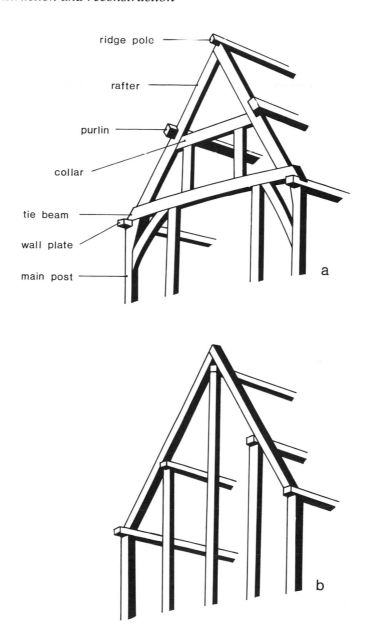

7. (a) A type of post and truss roof frame; (b) a roof supported by individual uprights.

('wigwam' and 'beehive' dwellings); and those where the wall and roof are differentiated. In the first group three fundamental types can be recognised (figure 8): (a) the conical (*wigwam*) form of rigid poles set firmly in the ground and lashed together at the top; (b) the *beehive* form of flexible poles set firmly in the ground and also lashed together at the top; (c) the domed 'beehive' form where flexible poles are fixed firmly at both ends. For those round-houses where the framing of the enclosing wall and the roof were distinct the methods of construction would have been comparable in a number of ways to those employed in building rectangular structures. A circular wall plate, made of intertwined withies or short lengths of timber joined together, would have spread the weight of the roof round the building. Experimental work at the Butser Archaeological Farm has shown that the rigidity of the roof could have been improved by a circular collar, of similar construction to the wall plate, a third of the way down from the apex of the roof. Stability would have been further enhanced by timbers set within and criss-crossing the roof space. In some rectangular buildings the same function was fulfilled by collars and tie beams, which connected with the principal rafters to form the roof truss. This type of construction relied on accurate jointing and pegging and may have developed during the iron age with the introduction of more sophisticated tool types, including the saw.

At the centre of some round-houses a post was erected, again presumably to enhance stability by keeping the apex of the roof in the correct position. A common feature in round-houses, whether of timber or stone-walled construction, was a ring of four or more posts, positioned some distance away from the wall. This type of structure is referred to as a double-ring round-house (figure 9). Within some larger circular buildings two concentric rings of posts, set some distance apart, were erected. These buildings are known as treble-ring round-houses. The post-rings appear to have acted in much the same way as the posts forming aisles or partitions in rectangular buildings, that is as supports for the roof, a loft and any upper floors, as well as differentiating areas according to function and social custom. In these houses the post-ring

8. 'Wigwam' and 'beehive' houses: (a) conical (wigwam), (b) beehive, (c) domed beehive. (After Gebremendhim.)

9. Developed forms of timber- and stone-built double-ring round-house compared. Dwellings of this type were constructed throughout much of Britain during the bronze and iron ages. (Reconstruction drawing by Frank Gardiner.)

was surmounted by a series of jointed timbers, known as a ring-beam, on which the rafters rested. As thatch was probably the commonest roofing material, it is likely that the roof pitch of most round-houses was slightly in excess of 45 degrees.

From the late bronze age and throughout the iron age square and rectangular post-built structures were constructed in association with round-houses. The majority are thought to be raised granaries, supported on four or six posts. A number of larger rectangular buildings dating from this period may well have functioned as dwellings.

Construction methods: stone

As with timber-framed buildings, a number of different techniques were used in the construction of stone-walled buildings, which largely depended on the type of stone available. The construction trench, so readily used as the method of foundation for many later buildings, appears not to have been considered necessary. In most cases the wall was built straight on to the ground. Where the ground was particularly soft, for example loose sand, a hollow was often excavated and the wall constructed as a revetment for a sunken or partly subterranean building.

Freestanding walls (those that did not act as a revetment) were often faced externally and internally with large stones. Separating the two faces, stone slabs, rubble (sometimes mixed with earth) or turf were used to form the core of the wall. As the majority of stone walls were built with rubble or boulders occurring on the site, the coursing of the faces tended to be very irregular and, without any bonding material, most walls could not have been constructed to any great height. In those areas where the stone could be split into blocks and slabs of a manageable size it was possible to construct high walls that were better coursed. The best-preserved examples of drystone houses dating from the prehistoric period in Britain are to be found in the north and west of Scotland. The tallest of these dwellings was the broch, which developed during the iron age. The sophisticated wall construction of these and other houses known as duns will be considered in chapter 5.

As in many timber-framed buildings dating from the neolithic, internal posts were erected to help support the roof and any upper floor or floors, as well as to divide the building into a number of rooms or compartments. As there was a lack of suitable timber in the Northern and Western Isles of Scotland by the later prehistoric period, the supports and partitions within many bronze and iron age round-houses were constructed of stone in the form of large slabs, or as a series of masonry piers abutting the enclosing wall, or as freestanding constructions.

It seems likely that the majority of stone-built houses had timber-framed roofs of similar construction to those wooden-built houses where wall and roof were differentiated. From the remains of neolithic funerary monuments on Orkney, it is clear that by this date the method of constructing corbelled roofs had been perfected. By this method successive courses of stone could be overlapped to produce a parabolic dome over a circular or square structure (figure 10). However, it is not clear to what extent this technique was used in house construction in prehistoric Britain. It probably depended to a large extent on the size and strength of the stone available and the area to be roofed. When corbelling was employed it was not always used to cover the whole roof. This is most clearly demonstrated by some iron age round-houses in the Northern and Western Isles of Scotland, known as wheelhouses and aisled round-houses, where the corbelling covered a series of rooms or compartments, separated by masonry piers, while the central area was presumably covered with a timber-framed roof. Where compartments or passages were smaller, these were often roofed by a series of slabs laid side by side.

Flooring and internal fixtures

Where stone was available, it was often used to pave house floors.

10. A cross-section through a corbelled stone-roofed structure.

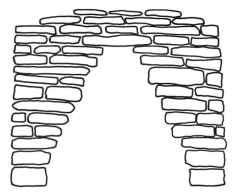

Earth, particularly clay, was also commonly used. Certain floors may have been covered with rushes or with woven rugs or skins, and possibly with wooden boards. Where partitions did not exist, different spaces were often signified by differences in flooring material, sometimes further emphasised by low stone kerbs or changes in floor height. In those houses where earthen or clay floor levels are preserved, it is noticeable from the build-up of deposits that floors of this type were resurfaced at regular intervals.

The most important feature in many prehistoric houses was the hearth. Usually placed at the centre of the building, it acted as the focal point around which all domestic activities took place. It was a source not only of heat but also of light. There is no evidence to suggest that windows were constructed in any of these buildings. With the exception of any vents for the smoke to escape, the only source of natural light would have been through the doorway or doorways. This light would have been even more severely restricted where the entrance to the house was through a covered passageway. Lamps, of clay or stone (figure 11), provided additional light.

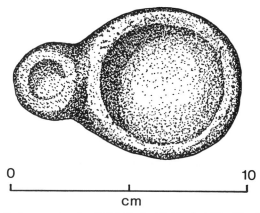

0   10
└────────────────────────┴────────────────────────┘
cm

11. A stone lamp from the iron age broch at Clickhimin, Shetland. (After Hamilton.)

12. House 1, Skara Brae, Orkney. The walls of these subterranean neolithic dwellings are surrounded by earlier midden deposits and accumulations of windblown sand. The walls of this house survive to a height of 2.5 metres.

Where available, stone was often used to edge hearths, storage pits, tanks and drains. The location of wells within the interior of numerous brochs clearly demonstrates the importance attached by the occupants to having an immediate supply of fresh water.

Much of the furniture and other fittings within prehistoric houses is likely to have been made of wood. However, there are instances, most notably the neolithic settlement at Skara Brae, where because of the lack of timber such fixtures and fittings were made of stone (figure 12).

4
Excavating prehistoric houses: developing techniques and changing perceptions

In the late nineteenth century there was a move to develop archaeology from an antiquarian pursuit into a scientific discipline. Excavation of archaeological sites up to this time had consisted largely of digging unsystematic holes in order to recover buried artefacts, and there was usually no attempt to record the deposits in which these objects lay. Consequently the contextual information, so important to archaeology, was lost for ever. The principal exponent of the new 'scientific' archaeology was General Pitt Rivers. The excavations directed by him were conducted like military operations, carried out by a workforce trained to distinguish differences in the colour and texture of archaeological deposits, which formed a stratigraphic sequence. Artefacts of significance were recorded where they were found, and their positions were marked on scaled plan and section drawings of the deposits and features excavated. Despite these methods, Pitt Rivers did not fully grasp the importance of stratigraphy in establishing the relative chronology of a site.

Unlike many of his predecessors and contemporaries, Pitt Rivers excavated a wide range of sites, including prehistoric settlements. In 1893 he systematically excavated the bronze age enclosed settlement at South Lodge, Wiltshire. The interior was stripped by digging a series of parallel trenches, up to a metre wide, which he excavated and backfilled in succession. But this method was not adequate to locate ill-defined features or all the small ones, such as post and stake holes, which cut into the chalk. Only one post hole was found during this investigation. This site was re-excavated in 1977-81 and it was found that this post hole was one of a group of thirteen forming the larger of two round-houses. Although Pitt Rivers recorded post-hole structures, many other archaeologists at this time believed that the normal type of prehistoric dwelling in lowland England was a covered pit (figure 13). This belief persisted into the twentieth century despite excavations undertaken on stone-built bronze age round-houses, such as those at Grimspound, by the Dartmoor Exploration Society in the 1890s, and the discovery and subsequent excavation of the iron age lake village at Glastonbury, Somerset.

Work started here in 1892, directed by Arthur Bulleid, who was soon to be joined by Harold St George Gray, an assistant of Pitt Rivers. This

13. A mythical pit dwelling. (Drawing by Frank Gardiner.)

settlement lay in the raised mire of the Somerset Levels, and the waterlogged conditions had preserved a whole range of structural and artefactual evidence. Excavations were very extensive; virtually the whole settlement, covering an area of about 1.4 hectares, was excavated over eleven seasons up to 1907. The site consisted of an artificial island largely composed of timber, mainly supporting small groups of circular buildings, which served as houses, stables, stores and workshops. These buildings consisted of a timber base surrounded by a wattle and daub wall; floors were of clay, renewed on a number of occasions as the structures sank into the soft, damp ground (figure 14).

Like the investigations carried out by Pitt Rivers, these excavations were conducted in a methodical manner, with structures and finds being described in detail. However, stratigraphic relationships between structures were still not fully appreciated, nor was the accurate recording of contextual information for artefact analysis.

In the south-west of Scotland at this time Robert Munro was concerned with the systematic excavation of crannogs (artificial island dwellings), discovered during the draining of shallow lochs. Munro's first excavation was carried out in 1878 at Lochlee, Strathclyde. He produced very

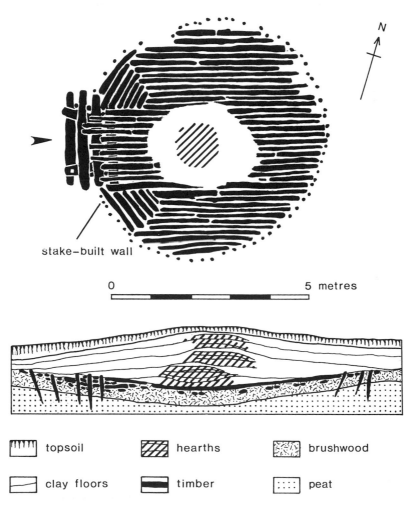

stake-built wall

0   5 metres

topsoil   hearths   brushwood

clay floors   timber   peat

14. Mound 74, Glastonbury iron age lake village. A plan of a stake-built round-house, constructed on a timber raft, with the remains of a clay floor and hearth. The section, at the same scale, shows how this structure was sealed by the floors of later buildings, many containing a central hearth. (After Coles and Coles.)

accurate measured plan and section drawings, which clearly demonstrate the complex construction of these buildings. What Munro did not realise and has been fully recognised only with the aid of scientific dating methods was that crannogs were frequently reoccupied over a considerable length of time and thus cannot be seen as single-period constructions. The excavations undertaken by Munro still form the basis for analysing crannogs in Scotland and have provided many of the details on which the reconstruction on the front cover is based.

Meanwhile, in other parts of Scotland, stone-built houses of prehistoric date also received considerable attention. Chief amongst them were the impressive iron age brochs. The normal method of excavation was to 'open up' the interiors by removing accumulations of soil and collapsed stonework. Any plan and section drawings of the deposits excavated were usually woefully inadequate, and the artefacts recovered often lacked a provenance. Many of the excavators also failed to understand the complex structural picture resulting from the additions and alterations to individual structures and settlement layouts over hundreds, and sometimes thousands, of years. Although there were exceptions, this situation did not significantly improve until after the Second World War.

In the 1930s the numbers of excavations undertaken on prehistoric settlements all over Britain increased dramatically. Two excavations undertaken in Wessex are worthy of particular note: Maiden Castle and Little Woodbury. The investigations at Maiden Castle, Dorset, were directed by Mortimer Wheeler between 1934 and 1937. This multi-period site consisted of a neolithic causewayed enclosure and funerary monument and an iron age hillfort with the remains of stone- and timber-built round-houses, as well as occupation in the Roman period. By this time Wheeler had established himself as an extremely skilful excavator capable of recording and analysing sites with a complex history. This he achieved by the controlled and systematic excavation of selected areas, making sure that the artefacts recovered could be related to the deposits from which they had come.

The excavations at the iron age enclosed settlement at Little Woodbury, Wiltshire, were conducted by Gerhard Bersu between 1938 and 1939. A large area of the site was examined by digging a series of alternate strips 4 to 5 metres wide. This exposed the tops of the features, such as pits and post holes, which had been cut into the bedrock. These features were then planned and sectioned in turn. By these methods, Bersu was able to work out the sequence of occupation and build up a detailed picture of life within this settlement. The recognition of substantial post-built round-houses on this site (figure 15) finally put paid to the idea that iron age people in lowland England existed as troglodytes.

After the Second World War the establishment of major programmes of research and rescue excavations went hand in hand with the continued development of excavation and recording techniques. With regard to the analysis of prehistoric houses, a number of important advances have been made since the late 1960s.

Before this time many of the timber-built round-houses of bronze and iron age date were thought to be small structures consisting of a single ring of post holes, with two outer post holes often marking the position of a projecting porch. However, the evidence of such small houses seemed to be at odds with that on some of the better-preserved sites. The evidence was re-examined and it was found that the majority of these structures were not small huts but quite substantial buildings, consisting of an internal post-ring and probably an outer stake-built wall — a type of building known as a double-ring round-house (figure 9). Because of the slight foundation, the outer wall often left no trace, having been easily destroyed by later ploughing.

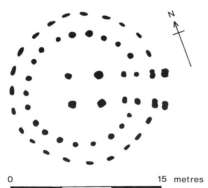

0   15 metres

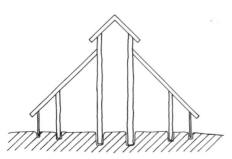

During the 1960s and 1970s archaeologists started to come to terms with the various processes that contributed to the formation, and subsequent alteration, of the archaeological record. Central to this 'new archaeology' was the belief that it was possible to interpret patterns of human behaviour from the stratigraphical, structural, artefactual and environmental evidence that remained. Important work has, for example, been carried out on differentiating types of refuse from archaeological deposits. Such research has major implications for settlement archaeology. By plotting the

15. Plan and reconstruction of House I at Little Woodbury, Wiltshire. As no floor deposits survived, it is unclear whether the four-post arrangement in the middle of the house was part of the structure. It may have been a totally separate construction, possibly the remains of a raised granary. The porch shown in plan has not been shown on the reconstruction drawing. (After Bersu.)

artefacts found in and around houses it is sometimes possible to deduce the types of activities which took place within these buildings. As well as examining the distribution of objects, archaeologists are now using scientific techniques to analyse the chemical and physical composition of floor levels and associated deposits, as a means of identifying different areas of domestic activity, or to distinguish houses from buildings of a similar plan that may have been used as byres or food stores. Such techniques have been used extensively during the excavation of prehistoric settlements at Fengate, Peterborough, Cambridgeshire.

Although necessarily selective, this brief review indicates how excavation and recording methods have developed and demonstrates how archaeological perceptions about the appearance of prehistoric dwellings have changed.

5
Prehistoric houses in Scotland and northern England

The remarkable state of preservation of many prehistoric settlements in northern Britain, and in the uplands and islands of Scotland in particular, has allowed archaeologists to recognise a diverse range of house types and styles. In this and the following two chapters the settlements selected for discussion will be those that are well-preserved and thoroughly investigated. As a result, there will be a tendency to focus on specific areas and periods.

Fourth to third millennium BC

The artefactual and environmental evidence indicates that it took many centuries for hunting communities in Britain to adopt a more sedentary way of life, based on agriculture. During the initial stages of the neolithic, domestic structures were temporary and probably movable constructions, reflecting the transitory lifestyle of these early farmers. The earliest domestic buildings which reflect long-term occupation so far discovered in northern Britain all date from around the mid fourth millennium BC. A substantial rectangular timber-framed building of this date has been excavated at Balbridie, Grampian (figure 17). It was divided by cross-walls into a number of rooms, and the foundation trenches, which were up to 2 metres deep, contained the remains of squared posts, 0.5 by 0.3 metres in cross-section. These timbers formed the frame of the building, and planks may have been placed between them to create the walls. It appears that this building, which probably stood 8 metres high, underwent a number of modifications before it was finally burnt down. Although its plan is similar in some respects to the contemporary timber-built funerary and ceremonial monuments, it is clear from the artefacts and the remains of cereals recovered that this building had a domestic function, either as a house of an important individual, or as a communal building. This structure probably stood alone, like the farmstead, consisting of two adjoining stone buildings, at Knap of Howar, Orkney, dated to the second half of the fourth millennium BC (figure 18). The larger of the two buildings at Knap of Howar was divided into two rooms by stone-slab partitions and seems to have been the focus of domestic activity; the smaller building of three rooms, also partitioned by stone slabs, was used as a store and workshop.

A settlement contemporary with Knap of Howar has been discovered at Loch Olabhat, North Uist. A farmstead on an artificial stone-built

16. Map of Scottish sites illustrated or mentioned in the text. Sites where the remains of prehistoric houses can be seen and which are noted in chapter 9 are indicated on the map by a square. 1 Scord of Brouster, 2 Stanydale, 3 Clickhimin, 4 Jarlshof, 5 Mousa, 6 Knap of Howar, 7 Midhowe, 8 Gurness, 9 Skara Brae, 10 Bu, 11 Dun Dornaigil, 12 Carn Liath, 13 Dun Carloway, 14 Loch Olabhat, 15 A' Cheardach Mhor, 16 A' Cheardach Bheag, 17 Kilpheder, 18 Dun Beag, 19 Dun Telve, 20 Dun Troddan, 21 Balbridie, 22 Carlungie, 23 Ardestie, 24 Edin's Hall, 25 Lochlee.

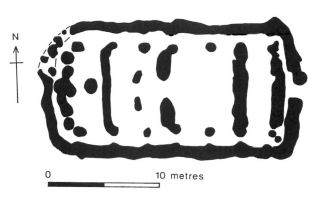

17. Plan of the foundations of a neolithic domestic structure at Balbridie, Grampian. (After Ralston.)

N

0   10 metres

island within the loch, connected to the shore by a wooden causeway, and later by one of stone, is very much like the crannogs of iron age date. Two major periods of early neolithic occupation have been identified. The earliest buildings — houses and ancillary structures — appear to be rectilinear or oval in shape and constructed of stone with wattle hurdles, while the final-phase structures, also rectilinear in plan, were more substantial, with walls constructed of stone and earth. The size and form of the island, with its inturned funnel-like entrance, has much in common with the contemporary funerary monuments in the region.

18. The early neolithic farmstead at Knap of Howar, Orkney. The walls, surrounded by earlier midden deposits and accumulations of windblown sand, stand to a height of 1.7 metres.

From around 3100 BC in Orkney there was a change in the settlement pattern from isolated farmsteads to small village-type settlements. This change was accompanied by others, such as the construction of impressive ceremonial and funerary monuments. These changes clearly point to the development of an hierarchical society, with a strong sense of group identity, but with a wide network of external contacts. The most famous and best-preserved of these 'villages' is Skara Brae, occupied between 3100 and 2450 BC. Two distinct periods of settlement are apparent, coinciding with differences in the size and construction of the houses (figure 19). Within all houses there was a central hearth surrounded by stone-lined beds (in the earlier houses these were built into the walls) and other furniture, including dressers, made of stone slabs (figure 12). These houses are not at all like the earlier dwellings at Knap of Howar and their design again seems to resemble the funerary architecture of the period. The internal arrangement of the houses at Skara Brae will be considered further in chapter 8.

By 2000 BC houses with a more oval plan were being constructed throughout the Northern Isles. At Scord of Brouster, Shetland, houses of this type, found in association with burial cairns and a field system, are comparable to those at the nearby con-temporary settlement at Stanydale, at the centre of which is a large building known as the Temple — probably a communal hall or the residence of an important individual.

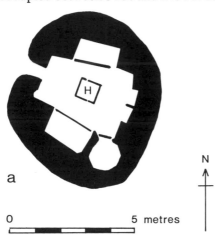

a

0   5 metres

N

H hearth

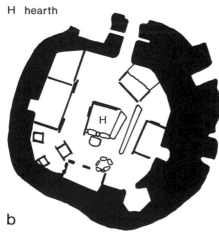

b

19. Plans of (a) earlier and (b) later houses at Skara Brae, Orkney. (After Clarke and Richards.)

Second to first millennium BC

Over much of northern Britain, with the principal exception of northern and western Scotland, domestic structures of neolithic date have so far remained largely undetected. It is not until the bronze age that settlements in other parts of Britain become more 'archaeologically visible', being preserved mainly on high ground, away from areas that remain intensively cultivated.

Throughout the bronze age in many of these upland areas houses occurred as single units, or as part of small settlements, located at the edge of contemporary fields. These houses were circular, with walls of timber or stone. The timber houses were often surrounded to some extent by a low bank of stone (a *ring-bank*). This stone was usually that cleared from land under cultivation. Within these structures a circle of posts was often positioned a short distance away from the wall, to take the main weight of the roof. These dwellings are an early form of the double-ring round-house.

By the mid first millennium BC the range of settlement types throughout northern Britain points to the development of an increasingly complex and hierarchical society. Over much of the region there was a tendency to enclose and fortify individual houses and homesteads (the residences of a single family), as well as larger communal settlements.

In eastern and southern Scotland and northern England a number of regionally distinctive house styles had appeared by this time. The most common type was the developed form of the double-ring round-house, with timber or stone-built walls and internal post-ring (figure 9). Within these houses, which were usually between 8 and 12 metres in diameter, the post-ring was positioned some distance away from the wall (often about 2 metres), irrespective of the overall size of the interior. In these later houses the post-ring not only functioned to support the roof but also appears to have been positioned so that the interior could be divided into two major functional areas: the central space with a hearth, the focus of communal domestic activity; and the outer area used for sleeping and storage, with wattle hurdles probably used extensively as partitions.

The location and differential sizes of houses within a settlement may provide a clue to the relative social standing of the occupants or to the activities carried out within. For example, in southern Scotland and northern England during the iron age homesteads were often dominated by a large double- or treble-ring round-house, between 10 and 18 metres in diameter, probably the residence of the head of the community. Within some of these buildings the outer zone or zones were emphasised by paved and sunken floors — the latter type also known as *ring-ditch* houses. A number of these large buildings may have functioned also as byres and communal food stores.

It is apparent that in Orkney and Shetland houses with an oval plan and cellular interior, like those at Scord of Brouster and Stanydale, continued to be constructed throughout the bronze age. Some, like those at Jarlshof, consisted of a central area with a hearth surrounded by a series of small rooms or compartments, divided by masonry piers, with the largest room furthest from the entrance, perhaps for the head of the household. At the time of the transition between the bronze and iron ages, around 700 BC, there was a very pronounced change in the form of houses in the Northern Isles — from oval to round-houses. Although there are some similarities with the bronze age dwellings, the space within these new houses tended to be more equally apportioned. Around the central communal area there was a series of small rooms of similar size, for sleeping and storage. These rooms tended to be divided by a series of masonry piers or stone slabs, radially placed, which also served as roof supports. Sometimes a ring of posts took the place of piers or stone slabs. In terms of both the internal planning and the utilisation of space these dwellings are similar to the contemporary double-ring round-houses constructed in other parts of Britain. The organisation of space within the iron age houses of northern Scotland will be discussed further in chapter 8.

In many parts of Scotland during the iron age those who held positions of power and authority tended to reflect their social standing by the construction of grand imposing defensive stone-built residences — the brochs and duns. According to the established classification of prehistoric settlements, duns vary in their construction from individual circular thick-walled houses and homesteads, with walls up to 3 metres high and about 4 metres wide, to larger communal settlements of hillfort proportions. Brochs, on the other hand, were individual circular dwellings with walls up to 6 metres wide. Some, but by no means all, were constructed as extremely tall tower houses, with walls in excess of 10 metres high.

The earliest dwellings displaying defensive characteristics have been found in the Northern Isles. The start of this process can be observed at Bu, Orkney (figure 20). The construction of this house, with its internal radial divisions, is dated to the sixth century BC. Subsequently the encircling wall was enlarged, not apparently to consolidate the existing structure, but to transform this modest farmhouse into a residence of some pretension.

Dun houses and brochs share a number of common features: their thick walls were wide enough to contain guard chambers, intramural cells, stairs and passageways. As the encircling wall of a broch rose from its thick base, it tapered, so reducing gravitational pressures and producing the distinctive 'cooling-tower' shape characteristic of the

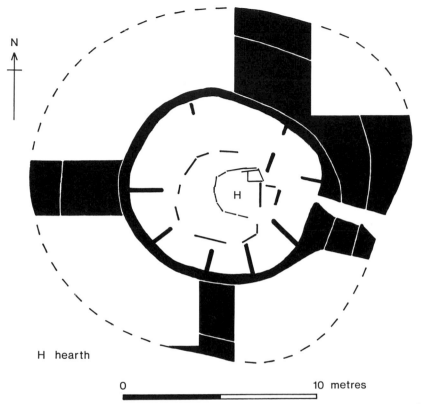

20. Plan of the early iron age radially divided round-house at Bu, Orkney. The sections of the encircling wall exposed during the archaeological excavation are shown in solid black. The initial construction included the middle section of the wall; the internal and external facings are considered to be later. Stone kerbs are also shown, used around the hearth and to help separate the central room from the radially divided peripheral area. (After Hedges.)

tallest brochs. The best-preserved of all the brochs is Mousa, Shetland, which survives to a height of 13 metres (figure 21). Within its walls a stairway still provides access to a gallery near the top of the structure. Stairs were similarly positioned in some duns to give access to the wall tops. The cavity wall construction employed in the building of many brochs and some dun houses appears to have acted as a technical device to lighten these extremely heavy walls, which might otherwise collapse under their own weight. In broch construction, cross-slabs spanned the cavities and joined the two parts of the wall together, thus providing access to internal galleries and a means of internal scaffolding. Vertical voids positioned at various points around the inner wall, especially over

21. The Broch of Mousa, Shetland.

doorways, also helped to lighten the load of the wall (figure 22).

Despite the amazing state of preservation of many brochs and dun houses, it is not entirely clear how such structures were roofed but, when these types are compared with other contemporary houses, conical roofs, covering the whole of the interior, seem the most likely. At Dun Telve, Highland Region (figure 22), a scarcement (a ledge around the inner wall face) 9 metres from floor level was probably designed to hold roofing timbers in place. Within this broch there is also a lower scarcement, 2 metres from the floor level. Scarcements about this height are a common feature in many brochs and with a ring of posts (for example within the broch at Dun Troddan, Highland Region) were used to support a timber gallery. Within the brochs of the Northern Isles and Caithness, radial divisions of large stone slabs, like the earlier roundhouse at Bu, acted with the scarcement to support a gallery of stone flags.

The arrangement of radial partitions also characterises the aisled round-houses and wheelhouses (figure 23), found throughout the Western Isles and on Shetland, which are dated to the closing centuries BC and the first few centuries AD. Externally, both these house types would have been far less imposing than the brochs and dun houses; in the

22. Part of the internal wall face of the broch at Dun Telve, Highland Region. Two vertical voids can be seen, bridged by slabs; the one on the left is situated over the entrance passage. The two scarcements can also be seen; the lower one corresponds to the top of the 2 metre ranging pole.

Western Isles they were constructed as subterranean dwellings, their walls revetting the soft sandy subsoil; and at Jarlshof, Shetland, where both types are represented, they lie within and next to the earlier broch. Internally, the principal difference between these two house types was the method of masonry pier construction: in the wheelhouses the piers abutted the encircling wall, while in the aisled round-houses the piers were freestanding, to create a slender 'aisle' between the pier and the wall face (figure 24).

Another distinctive prehistoric house type found in Scotland is the crannog (see cover illustration). Dating from the early iron age, these artificial islands, which occupy the shallow waters of numerous lochs and estuaries, continued to be constructed and frequently reoccupied until the medieval period. Pile-driven stakes with horizontal timbers, often of oak, were used to define and provide a framework for the island. Within this framework stone, brushwood, turf and other organic materials were dumped to provide a solid base. A timber causeway was frequently built to connect the crannog to the shore. On top of the substructure a timber-framed round-house was constructed, of a similar size and internal design to the double- and treble-ring round-houses considered previously. It would also seem that crannogs had close structural affinities to the duns and brochs that occupied small naturally occurring islands within the lochs of the Western Isles and Shetland. In terms of their position and size and the resources required for their construction, it is clear that crannogs, brochs and duns were the residences of important members of the local iron age community.

The early first millennium AD
Following the Roman conquest of Britain in the first century AD,

23. Wheelhouse 1, within the iron age settlement at Jarlshof, Shetland. The walls stand nearly to their full original height of 3 metres.

much of Scotland and northern England remained outside the principal area of Roman domination. Life seems to have continued much as before for many of the native tribes, with the exception of those who had political and economic contact with the Roman world. In those areas where such ties developed the pressures brought to bear on these

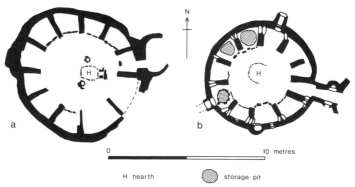

24. Plans of (a) a wheelhouse at A' Cheardach Mhor, South Uist, and (b) an aisled round-house at Kilpheder, South Uist. Lintel stones are shown in outline. In both houses stone kerbs were used around the hearth and to help separate the central room from the radially divided peripheral area. (After Young and Richardson [a] and Lethbridge [b].)

tribes were ultimately to have an effect on family life, resulting in changes to the domestic architecture. In north-eastern England and southern Scotland, for example, there is a noticeable progression during the first and second centuries AD from large timber-built round-houses, with central communal spaces, to smaller timber and stone-built dwellings. Differences in the internal design of these new houses and the lack of space for the occupants to participate in communal activities indicate a significant reordering of domestic relations at this time. Settlements of this period consisting of small houses, some with two adjoining round/oval rooms, and associated souterrains (underground food-stores) can be seen at Ardestie and Carlungie, Tayside.

Excavations of native farmsteads in Cumbria have revealed that by the late third century AD the traditionally built round-house was being replaced by buildings of Romanised character, notably rectangular timber-framed structures, some with stone footings and possibly stone-slab roofs.

Developments centring on the broch settlements of Orkney and Caithness may also have resulted from the contacts which were established with the Romans. Here, the internal structure of brochs occupied at this time changed from the radial pattern, established and reproduced over many centuries, to a series of distinct apartments, where there was no communal centre. This is most clearly demonstrated by the broch at Midhowe, Orkney, where the interior was divided by a central wall of sandstone slabs standing 2.4 metres high. This broch, like many others in Orkney and Caithness, dominated the surrounding contemporary settlement, composed of small conjoined, irregularly shaped houses, such as those at Gurness, Orkney (figure 25).

25. The iron age broch settlement at Gurness, Orkney. The entrance way, with the remains of iron age houses on either side, leads to the broch at the centre of the settlement. This broch was probably never as tall as Mousa, Dun Telve or Dun Troddan.

6
Prehistoric houses in Wales and the south-west of England

Fourth to third millennium BC

Of all the neolithic houses so far excavated in Wales and the south-west of England none has survived to the degree of those in northern Scotland. The majority of the evidence for settlements of this period over much of Britain consists of scatters of artefacts disturbed by the plough or the truncated remains of features cut into the subsoil, such as pits, stake and post holes. Only rarely have complete plans of neolithic houses been preserved and, even where they have survived, they have tended not to be very substantial or well founded.

The earliest houses to be discovered in Wales and the south-west of England date from the first half of the fourth millennium BC. Most form part of individual, isolated farmsteads, each occupied by a small social group. At this early date in southern and central England people were also beginning to create larger settlements and communal centres, enclosed by discontinuous lengths of bank and ditch or stone rampart. These sites are known collectively as causewayed enclosures. Despite the difference in settlement type, the majority of these early neolithic houses appear to be reasonably similar. Indeed, apart from variations in wall foundation, which would seem largely to reflect differences in subsoil or rock type and local topography, little change in the basic house form is detectable throughout the duration of the neolithic in these two areas.

Houses were invariably small and, although not all of those excavated have complete ground plans surviving, they appear to be of comparable size to the neolithic houses at Knap of Howar and Skara Brae, Orkney. All are rectangular or sub-rectangular in plan, usually consisting of post-built or stake-built walls, sometimes consolidated by stone or founded on stone footings, with posts helping to support the roof and dividing the interior (figure 27). Within the neolithic fortified complex at Carn Brea, Cornwall, stake-built houses, rebuilt and modified on a number of occasions, occupied separate, partly purpose-built terraces, similar to those at Helman Tor, another contemporary enclosed settlement also in Cornwall.

Some neolithic houses have survived only because later prehistoric structures, which have sealed the more ancient and fragile remains, were built on the same site. At Trelystan, Powys, two late neolithic stake-built houses were found beneath bronze age burial monuments

26. Map of sites in England and Wales illustrated or mentioned in the text. Sites where the remains of prehistoric houses can be seen and which are noted in chapter 9 are indicated by a square. 1 Halangy Down, 2 Nornour, 3 Little Bay, 4 Carn Euny, 5 Chysauster, 6 Gwithian, 7 Trethellan Farm, Newquay, 8 Carn Brea, 9 Trethurgy, 10 Helman Tor, 11 Shaugh Moor, 12 Merrivale, 13 Holne Moor, 14 Grimspound, 15 Haldon, 16 Brean Down, 17 Glastonbury, 18 South Cadbury, 19 Maiden Castle, 20 Hod Hill, 21 South Lodge, 22 Down Farm, 23 Little Woodbury, 24 Bowman's Farm, 25 Broom Hill, 26 Danebury, 27 Rams Hill, 28 Silchester, 29 Belle Tout, 30 Gorhambury, 31 Skeleton Green, 32 Lofts Farm, 33 'Boudicca's Palace', Thetford, 34 Fengate, 35 Flag Fen, 36 Lismore Fields, Buxton, 37 Ty Mawr, 38 Din Lligwy, 39 Cae'r-mynydd, 40 Moel y Gaer, 41 Trelystan, 42 Castell Henllys, 43 Stackpole Warren, 44 Mount Pleasant, 45 Whitton.

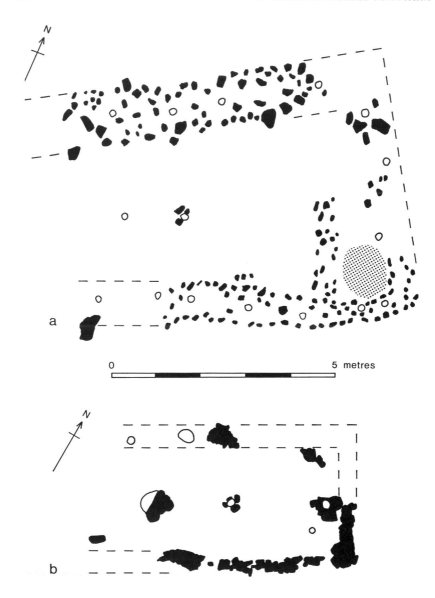

27. Incomplete plans of neolithic houses at (a) Haldon, Devon, and (b) Mount Pleasant, West Glamorgan. The remains of the stone walls are shown in solid black, post holes as open circles, and the hearth in the house at Haldon is indicated by the stippled area. (After Clark [a] and Savory [b].)

(figure 28). The relatively light foundation of these structures, their association with artefacts introduced from adjoining lowland areas and the evidence of wild, rather than cultivated plant species, has led to the suggestion that they were inhabited seasonally, while sheep or cattle grazed summer pastures.

Second to first millennium BC

By the beginning of the second millennium BC house forms had changed from rectilinear to circular. The foundations of early double-ring round-houses with post- and stake-built walls have been found within the coastal sands of Stackpole Warren, Dyfed, and at Gwithian, Cornwall. The formation of sand dunes also helped preserve the early bronze age stone-built settlements on the Isles of Scilly, such as Little Bay and Nornour. Both these settlements consisted of a series of conjoined round and oval structures, some containing radial partition walls, like those that characterised iron age round-houses of northern and western Scotland. Both these settlements were occupied over a considerable period, and, in the case of Nornour, possibly until the early first millennium AD.

Excavations undertaken at Brean Down, Somerset, following erosion by the sea of the sand cliffs, revealed one of the best-preserved bronze age settlement sites in southern England. Part of an oval stone building, constructed around the middle of the second millennium BC, was succeeded by round-houses that were of combined stone and timber construction, terraced into the dunes and surrounded by eavesdrip gullies. One of the principal activities undertaken within these houses was the production of salt from sea water. Around 1000 BC these

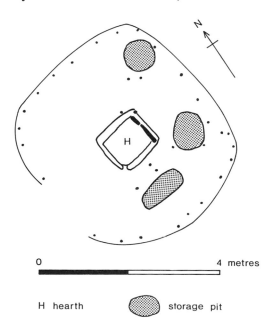

0   4 metres

H hearth   storage pit

28. Plan of one of the later neolithic stake-built structures found at Trelystan, Powys. The outward slant of the stake holes of the wall indicates that this structure was probably of 'beehive' construction. (After Britnell.)

houses were abandoned and thereafter enveloped by the surrounding dunes.

The concentrations of upstanding prehistoric stone-built settlements and of burial and ceremonial monuments existing on the upland moors of the south-west of England have long attracted archaeologists. On Dartmoor, for example, two principal types of permanent settlement dating to the bronze age have been recognised: groups of houses enclosed by a thick stone wall (known locally as pounds), for example at Grimspound, and open settlements, where houses were built near to field boundaries and major property divisions known as reaves, such as those at Merrivale. Extensive archaeological investigations at Holne Moor and Shaugh Moor have provided an invaluable insight into the development of the later prehistoric landscape on Dartmoor, together with the living conditions of bronze age communities. At Holne Moor boundary fences associated with post- and stake-built round-houses, some with an internal post-ring, were constructed around 1700/1600 BC. Probably within a generation many of the fences and timber houses had been replaced by boundaries and round-houses constructed of stone. The internal sizes of these new buildings (most between 4 and 7 metres in diameter) were comparable with the former structures that stood on the site, and also with the contemporary establishment of stone-walled houses, for example at Shaugh Moor. The internal layout of these houses, with a circle of posts close to the wall to support the roof, is similar to the early double-ring round-houses that were being constructed in Scotland and northern England at this time. Stone-walled houses of this type, dating to the bronze age, have been found throughout the south-west of England. In addition to these houses, another type of domestic structure of bronze/iron age date has been recognised on the upland moors — small circular stone constructions up to 3 metres in diameter internally. These appear to be shielings, the temporary abodes of herdsmen and shepherds.

At Trethellan Farm, Newquay, Cornwall, excavations have revealed a well-preserved bronze age settlement consisting of a linear arrangement of wooden circular structures, occupied between the fifteenth and thirteenth centuries BC. On this site the structural remains, combined with the artefactual and botanical evidence, suggest a distinction between the principal dwelling houses, often larger and more sophisticated in their design, and the other buildings, which appear to have served as ancillary structures.

House types seem to change very little throughout much of the first millennium BC in the south-west of England. Round-houses with stone or timber walls continued to be constructed, although they tended to be somewhat larger, on average, than those constructed during the previous millennium. Many of these later houses contained a ring of posts, positioned not only to support the roof, but also to partition the interior for various activities.

Little can be said with certainty about house types of the second millennium BC in Wales, mainly because of the poor survival of settlements and the lack of closely datable domestic artefacts from this period. In some regions, however, it seems likely that settlements occupied during the iron age and Roman period originated in the bronze age.

In recent years major programmes of archaeological excavation have been undertaken within the hillforts and smaller enclosed and defended settlements that dominated much of the Welsh landscape in the iron age. Because of the truncating effects of later activity on many of these sites, and the extensive use of wood for wall construction, usually only the foundations of buildings have survived.

Extensive excavations at Moel y Gaer, Clwyd, have revealed three distinct periods of later prehistoric settlement, beginning probably in the early iron age. This initial period of occupation consisted of a large hilltop settlement enclosed by a palisade and composed of double-ring round-houses with projecting porches and stake-built walls set in shallow ring-grooves (most of these shallow foundations had been destroyed by later activity) (figure 29a). During the fourth century BC a rampart was constructed to replace the palisade and the interior was completely reorganised, giving the appearance of a much more planned settlement, with rows of four-post raised granaries and stake-built round-houses

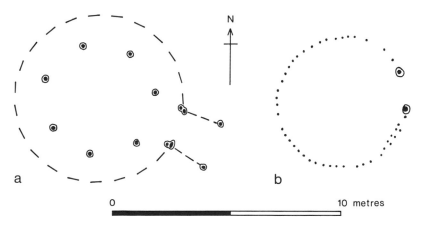

29. Plans of iron age houses at Moel y Gaer, Clwyd: (a) the earlier double-ring dwellings; (b) the later stake-built houses. The walls of the earlier houses were set in shallow trenches, most having been completely destroyed by later occupation. The position of these wall trenches is suggested by the post holes forming the porch. (After Guilbert.)

30. Reconstructed round-houses within the iron age hillfort at Castell Henllys, Dyfed.

without an internal post-ring (figure 29b). This settlement seems to have been short-lived, but later in the iron age the site was again reoccupied and new defences were built, enclosing a series of rectangular timber-framed buildings apparently founded on sill beams. Although precise reasons cannot be given for the marked changes in building types occurring on the site, it seems probable that they relate to differences in activity, organisation or social standing of the occupants.

Throughout the pre-Roman iron age in Wales, like many other parts of Britain, timber-built round-houses, of plank, post and stake construction, often set within a ring-groove, continued to be built. Many of the larger houses were of the double-ring type. However, excavation and subsequent reconstruction of the structures at Castell Henllys, Dyfed (figure 30), has shown that an internal post-ring was not always necessary to help support the roof, even for buildings 10 metres in diameter.

In north-west Wales round-houses with stone walls seem particularly common. Unenclosed house groups at Ty Mawr, Holyhead Mountain, Anglesey, Gwynedd, were occupied during the iron age and possibly throughout much of the Roman period. Excavations of other iron age and Roman period native settlements in the area have shown that in some cases later stone houses overlie the remains of earlier iron age circular dwellings.

The early first millennium AD

During this period in parts of Wales and the south-west of England pronounced changes in the form and internal layout of domestic buildings occur. These changes can be seen as part of the general process of Romanisation but may also relate to the social and economic upheaval created by the Roman forces.

In the south-west of England, and most notably in Cornwall, the round-house, the long-established dwelling type, had been replaced by houses of a very different form during the early centuries AD. These new houses were built to an oval plan, often with stone walls, but sometimes incorporating timber posts (figure 31), and this type includes the more sizable and elaborate courtyard houses. These dwellings are so called because of the large central area, commonly assumed to be an open courtyard, surrounded by a range of smaller chambers or rooms. Some of the small chambers contained within the walls probably had corbelled, slab-covered roofs. The principal room, which was invariably

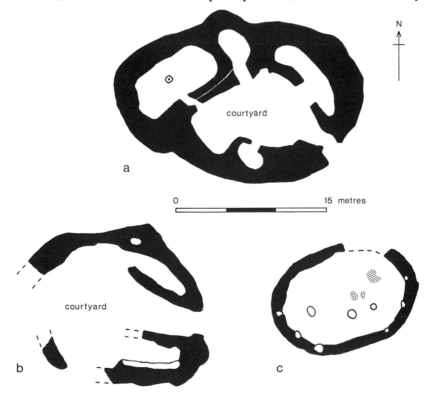

31. Plans of native Roman-period houses in Cornwall: (a) Courtyard House 4 at Chysauster; (b) Courtyard House II at Carn Euny (plan incomplete); (c) Trethurgy House T2. Post holes are shown in outline and stippled areas indicate the positions of hearths/ovens. (After Hencken [a], Christie [b] and Quinnell [c].)

round or oval, situated opposite and furthest from the entrance, would have had a timber-framed roof (figure 32). The side chambers, depending on their size and shape, were used for sleeping, storage or as byres. Courtyard houses have a seemingly very localised distribution, being found on the Land's End peninsula and the Isles of Scilly. They normally occur as individual farmsteads, such as Carn Euny, although larger settlements, for example Chysauster, were also constructed.

At the same time as the developments in the south-west of England, house and settlement forms were also beginning to change in north-west Wales. In this region homesteads consisting of round and rectangular stone buildings set around a courtyard, and enclosed by a stone wall (figure 33), were now being built. Some of these homesteads bear a superficial resemblance to the Cornish courtyard houses. Although the form of these enclosed homesteads probably developed from indigenous settlement types, the inclusion of rectangular buildings

32. Reconstruction of a courtyard house based on House 5 at Chysauster, Cornwall, by Frank Gardiner.

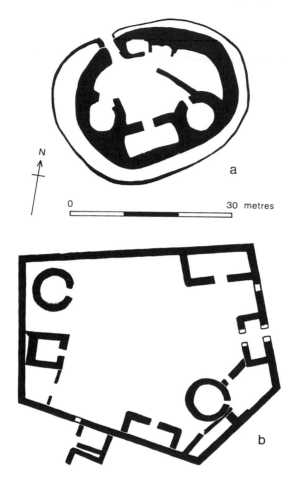

33. Plans of two Roman-period enclosed native settlements: (a) Cae'r-mynydd, Gwynedd; (b) Din Lligwy, Anglesey, Gwynedd. (After Griffiths [a] and RCAM Wales [b].)

certainly indicates Roman influence.

In south-eastern Wales the processes of Romanisation were more quickly and keenly felt. In terms of building styles, this was clearly demonstrated at Whitton, West Glamorgan. Excavation revealed a farmstead consisting of timber-framed round-houses surrounded by earthwork defences, established in the mid first century AD. Within a hundred years this settlement had been replaced by rectangular stone buildings round a courtyard — a characteristic Roman villa-farm.

7
Prehistoric houses in south-east and central England

Sixth to fifth millennium BC

Structural features associated with occupation sites of the mesolithic period have been found in various parts of the British Isles. Because of the transitory way of life of these hunting communities, many camps were temporary, consisting of lightly founded and probably portable dwellings. As the remains of these structures were ephemeral in nature and are often poorly preserved, it is usually very difficult to reconstruct their form. However, at two sites near Romsey, Hampshire — Broom Hill and Bowman's Farm — the remains of late mesolithic structures which appear to have been more than temporary dwellings have been discovered; indeed, they have been claimed as the oldest houses so far discovered on the British mainland. The Broom Hill dwelling was occupied around 7000 BC and consisted of an oval setting of posts, which surrounded a sunken area with a hearth towards one end (figure 34). At Bowman's Farm a group of four roughly circular post-built structures was found; they appear to be closely comparable with the earlier mesolithic houses discovered at Mount Sandel, County Londonderry — all possibly of the 'beehive' type (figure 8). The initial dating of the Bowman's Farm settlement indicated that it was occupied around 4800 BC.

Fourth to third millennium BC

The majority of neolithic houses discovered in central and south-eastern England tend to be small rectilinear structures of wooden construction, comparable in their size and form to other houses dating from this period found in other parts of the country. Many are poorly preserved, providing little information about construction techniques or the use of internal space. In 1984-7 excavations in advance of de-

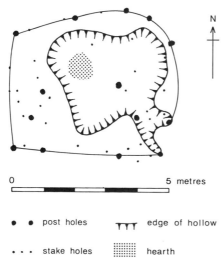

● ● post holes	⊤⊤⊤ edge of hollow
. . . stake holes	▦ hearth

34. Plan of a mesolithic dwelling at Broom Hill, Hampshire. (After O'Malley.)

0   5 metres

velopment at Lismore Fields, Buxton, Derbyshire, led to the chance discovery of a well-preserved neolithic settlement, occupied between the early and mid fourth millennium BC. The houses were rectangular and post-built (figure 35); the post-pipes and stone packing within the post holes indicate that the major structural uprights had been cleft or trimmed. Against these posts wattle hurdles covered with daub or planks were probably fixed. Foundation trenches and post holes mark the position of internal partition walls and roof supports — gable-ended or hipped roofs are both likely. The smaller house, Building II, appears less elaborate in its plan than Building I, consisting of two equal-sized rooms, with an entrance in the middle of the eastern wall. It is unclear whether Building I was two separate contemporary structures of equal proportions, each similar to Building II, or whether one half of the structure had been extended at a later date. Both halves of this building contained centrally placed hearths.

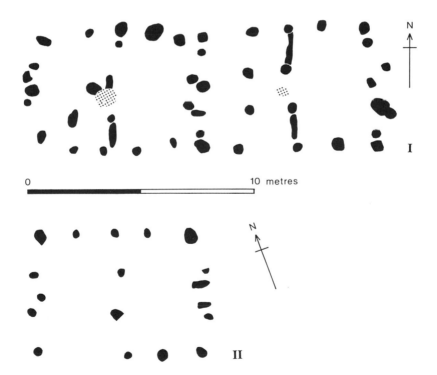

35. Plans of neolithic houses at Lismore Fields, Buxton, Derbyshire. The stippled areas indicate the positions of hearths. (After Garton.)

Second to first millennium BC

The development of housing during much of this period is essentially similar to that in Wales, south-west and northern England and southern Scotland. Early bronze age houses, like their neolithic predecessors, have tended to elude detection by the archaeologist. Slight remains of domestic structures of this date have been found at Belle Tout, East Sussex, where rectilinear and circular forms are represented. The nature of the foundations of such buildings indicates that many contemporary settlements have probably been obliterated by later cultivation. In some cases traces of the foundations, where they do survive, can be easily missed, because of their ephemeral nature, or assumed to be of natural origin, as happened within the bronze age enclosure at Rams Hill, Oxfordshire. Here, small circular features that cut into the chalk were initially considered to be root holes; some have been re-examined and are now thought to be the remains of stake-built structures.

During the later bronze age, from around the middle of the second millennium BC, a period of intensive farming in many parts of south-eastern and central England was marked by the establishment of extensive and planned field systems. Often small groups of houses were situated within embanked enclosures or alongside field boundaries, preservation of such structures being enhanced by their association with these earthworks. By this date the round-house had become the principal dwelling type. Some had a wall frame of posts interspersed with wattle hurdles covered with daub and surmounted by a wall plate, which spread the weight of the roof round the building. In others the main weight of the roof was carried on a ring-beam connected to an inner circle of posts, thus dividing the floor space into two distinct zones. The distinctions made between such buildings and how this may relate to the organisation of the household will be considered in chapter 8. Long rectangular buildings of later bronze age date, associated with round-houses, have been found on several sites in southern England. Those at Down Farm, Dorset, and Lofts Farm, Essex, may have had a living area at one end, with a barn or byre at the other.

The Peak District is particularly rich in the remains of bronze age funerary and ceremonial monuments, as well as the associated field systems which still cover many square kilometres of the gritstone moors. Until very recently the houses of the people who created this prehistoric landscape remained largely unnoticed. Detailed topographical surveys of some of these field systems have revealed the probable sites of small groups of circular timber-framed buildings, defined mainly by banks of stone cleared from the fields or smaller cultivation plots. These structures are superficially similar to the contemporary houses in Scotland and northern England.

Leading on from the later bronze age and throughout the iron age a complex settlement pattern emerges, dominated by hillforts, embanked and unenclosed farmsteads and nucleated villages. This range of settlements points to a complex hierarchical society, where wealth and political status are seen to relate to the control of agricultural land and other natural resources. A variety of house types has been recognised throughout south-east and central England during the first millennium BC. However, there appears to be no major distinction in house forms corresponding to the different types of settlement. Indeed, on the basis of house plans alone, it is often difficult to come to a firm conclusion about the relative social standing of the occupants.

The interiors of numerous hillforts throughout the region have been partially excavated. Many were used later for cultivation and as a consequence only the fragments of foundations of buildings tend to survive. At Danebury, Hampshire, prolonged and intensive occupation, coupled with the rebuilding of the defences, has sealed and preserved the foundations of many buildings, their floor levels and associated external deposits (figure 36). Occupation during the iron age lasted for about five hundred years, starting in the sixth century BC. The most common type of house averaged 6-7 metres in diameter and was built of stakes; some of the earliest were set within a ring-groove, but by the third century BC this technique appears to have been largely superseded by one where the individual stakes were placed in small holes created by a crowbar-like implement. In addition to these dwellings, post-built as well as plank-built houses were constructed. Door posts of all round-houses were deeply set in holes about 2 metres apart, sometimes connected to a wooden sill beam that lay in a narrow trench. Chalk was frequently used in the construction of paths to the houses and also in the creation of house floors. Hearths and bread ovens were frequently found in the houses and some also contained storage pits. The later stake-built dwellings, where the poles were driven or set in individual holes, are very similar in plan to the contemporary houses at Glastonbury lake village (figure 14) and the hillforts at South Cadbury, Somerset, and Moel y Gaer, Clwyd (figure 29b). Two distinctive building techniques can be postulated from the foundations of these stake-built houses: the use of a wall plate to separate the wall and roof, and a 'beehive' type structure, where the wall and roof were of one construction (figure 8). The use of coppiced poles to construct these buildings does not necessarily imply that large timber was in short supply. At Danebury, like other contemporary settlements, supplies of bulk timber must have been available for the construction of the numerous four-post and six-post raised granaries.

Throughout Wessex and the upper Thames valley, in hillforts, villages

36. One of the round-houses in the process of excavation within the iron age hillfort at Danebury, Hampshire. The circle of stake holes marks the position of the wattle-built wall, with post holes and beam slots of the doorway in the foreground. The two half-excavated storage pits are contemporary with the house. (Copyright Danebury Archaeological Trust.)

and farmsteads of iron age date, many of the principal houses were of a more substantial construction, averaging 10-12 metres in diameter. Most were of the double-ring type, with the surrounding wall, often of post and hurdle construction, set in holes or trenches (figure 37). Smaller and lighter-founded structures, of stake or post construction, have also been recognised where the conditions for preservation were favourable. In low-lying situations, and in particular where the subsoil is impermeable, penannular storm-water drainage gullies were often dug around the houses. On those sites that have been severely affected by later ploughing, these deeply excavated features may be all that is left to signify the sites of former buildings. In the west of the region, where stone was readily available, some buildings were founded on dwarf stone walls. Within the hillfort at Maiden Castle, Dorset, round-houses with stone and rubble walls co-existed with circular houses of timber-framed construction.

To the north and east of Wessex and the upper Thames valley the basic structural repertoire noted above appears to have been repeated with little variation throughout much of the iron age.

First century BC to the mid first century AD

During this period iron age communities in the south-east of England were developing strong economic and political ties with the Romanised Celtic tribes on the continent and with Rome itself. An expanding system of market exchange, fanning out from the core area in the south-east, and increasing Romanisation soon had an effect on all levels of iron age society in this part of the country. Administrative and financial control was now centred on the newly created planned settlements known as *oppida*.

Fundamental aspects of life quickly changed, including the introduction of coinage, the mass importation of luxury goods, the manufacture of new types of personal and household items, and new distinctive forms of domestic architecture. At Silchester, Hampshire, a settlement consisting of round-houses, dating to the mid first century BC, was transformed around 20 BC into the *oppidum* of *Calleva Atrebatum*, later to become an important Roman town. The *oppidum* was of a very different character to the former settlement, with a rectilinear pattern of cobbled streets separating a series of fenced plots containing small

37. A large double-ring round-house being reconstructed at Butser Archaeological Farm, Hampshire. The reconstruction is based on the excavated remains of an iron age settlement in Wessex.

rectangular timber-framed buildings. Similar types of structures have been found in the other *oppida* and high-status settlements throughout the south-east of England. At Skeleton Green, Hertfordshire, a settlement of small rectangular houses, consisting of one or two rooms (figure 38), was established during the final decade of the first century BC. The main structural timbers of these buildings were set in holes and trenches or connected to sill beams laid directly on the ground. Wattle and daub panels were fixed between the framing and a variety of materials, including cobbles and rammed chalk, were used in the construction of floors. At Gorhambury, also in Hertfordshire, a comparable range of contemporary buildings formed part of a farmstead. During the first and second centuries AD these buildings were replaced and a villa-farmhouse constructed. Similar structural sequences have also been discovered during the excavation of other Roman villas in the area.

In the rest of southern and central England, where there was little or no direct contact with the continent before the Roman invasion in AD 43, there appears to be little change in domestic architecture during the late iron age. It is interesting, and somewhat significant, that the large and impressive enclosed native settlement of the late pre-Roman and early Roman period at Thetford, Norfolk, known as 'Boudicca's Palace' should be dominated by large double-ring round-houses — a structural type of considerable antiquity.

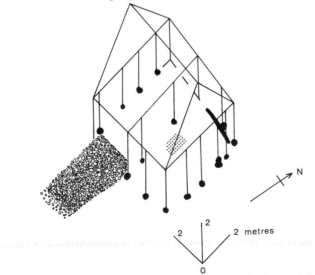

38. Axonometric plan, with the wall posts and roof projected, of one of the late iron age houses (VII) at Skeleton Green, Hertfordshire. The stippled area represents the hearth and a cobbled path led up to the house. (After Partridge.)

8
Exploring the social foundations of prehistoric houses

The nuclear family (mother, father and dependent children) that typifies much of modern British society is not necessarily the normal domestic structure of all the world's cultures. The household may, for example, be based on larger family groups, where men have more than one wife (polygamy) or share wives (polyandry). It is usual today for a nuclear family to occupy a single dwelling, whereas the members of an extended family often live in separate houses, segregated on the basis of age, gender or status. It is likely that the family structure of our prehistoric ancestors changed with time and may also have differed between one region and another. Such fundamental social relationships will have a direct bearing on the planning and layout of settlements and individual dwellings.

Any archaeological study that seeks to discern the organisation of family life from the excavated evidence is fraught with difficulties. However, several attempts have been made to examine the family structure of later prehistoric communities in southern England from the remains of settlements. The most widely accepted studies concern those living during the later bronze age. There are indications that during this period each family group occupied two round-houses in close proximity. On the basis of size, form and associated contemporary artefacts, it is suggested that the larger, more substantial houses were the major residential units, where eating, toolmaking and weaving were carried out. The majority of the smaller buildings appear to have been used as stores and for the preparation of food. It is not clear to what extent these tasks reflect the sexual division of labour, although it has been suggested that cooking and weaving may have been largely the concern of women. During the iron age there appears to have been a gradual transformation in the organisation of the household, with all members of a family tending to reside in a single large round-house.

Using anthropological studies as a base, archaeologists have tried to estimate the sizes of prehistoric communities from the remains of settlements, particularly in relation to floor space. Statistical formulae have been devised, but the nature of the archaeological evidence and the differences in social organisation from one culture to another make it extremely difficult to estimate the number of people inhabiting a prehistoric settlement at any given time.

There is a growing realisation amongst archaeologists that the theoretical and analytical approaches devised by anthropologists, sociologists and architects for the examination of recent and contemporary structures are applicable to some extent to the study of ancient settlements and houses. Such approaches are concerned with the deep-rooted responses by people to the physical environment and to their social or psychological needs. These inherited principles of human behaviour (which apply to all cultures, past and present) have influenced the form and layout of buildings and settlements.

The scale and external appearance of a building may convey much to the rest of the community about the social standing and pretensions of the occupants or about the types of activities carried out within. However, the purpose of a building is best understood by examining the arrangement, size and shape of internal spaces, created and modified in relation to the requirements of particular activities, but also according to social attitudes and beliefs. The order of internal spaces will reflect and also reinforce relations between people according to their age, gender and social standing. In the case of houses, this will also include the relationship between the occupants and those who enter as visitors, emphasised by differences in private and communal space. In some societies the space within the house will be strictly controlled, the rules observed having acquired symbolic meaning through centuries of tradition. Living spaces may, for example, be apportioned and orientated to reflect values concerning the daily and seasonal cycles of life, related to the positions of the major heavenly bodies — cosmology.

The well-preserved remains of prehistoric settlements in Scotland provide some of the best opportunities to assess some of the underlying social reasons that shaped the dwellings of this period. The later neolithic houses of Orkney, such as those at Skara Brae (figures 12 and 19), all have a similar internal structure formed by the cruciform positioning of the stone furniture: box-beds on either side of a central square hearth, with a dresser at the rear of the house, opposite the entrance. Recent analysis has pointed to the probable significance of the consistent design of these houses. The central position of the hearth was of great importance as it maximised the radiation of heat and light, allowed smoke to escape through the apex of the roof and kept the fire away from any combustible furnishings. The continued accuracy in the positioning of hearths in relation to other parts of these houses suggests that they also acted as the symbolic focus of domestic life. The orientation of the hearth, dresser and entrance was very carefully chosen, invariably aligned on a south-east/north-west axis. This alignment characterises many of the chambered tombs built by these people. This fundamental aspect of planning the houses of the living and of the dead corresponds to their orientation on the midsummer sunrise and sunset

— an important symbolic landmark in the yearly cycle.

Recent research on bronze and iron age settlements in southern England has suggested that the organisation of living space within houses and the orientation of entrances may have been linked to cosmological beliefs, as well as practical considerations. Doorways commonly faced east, perhaps symbolically orientated on the rising sun, and avoiding the prevailing winds. The intensity of natural light entering through a doorway (in buildings where there are presumed to have been no windows), together with light from the hearth and lamps, probably had a profound effect on the order and location of household activities.

The arrangement of space related to points of access and exit is an essential consideration in the planning of any building or settlement. Within a building, space can be categorised into two basic types: spaces that have 'defined' functions — rooms together with smaller compartments including cupboards; 'transitional spaces' — porches, halls, stairways and the like, which permit direct access into defined areas. These different types of space can be mapped out using a flow diagram to show how access, whether in an individual structure or a complex of

39. Plan of the two conjoined iron age wheelhouses/aisled round-houses at A' Cheardach Bheag, South Uist. (After Fairhurst.) The access diagram provides a graphical representation of the arrangement of space within these dwellings.

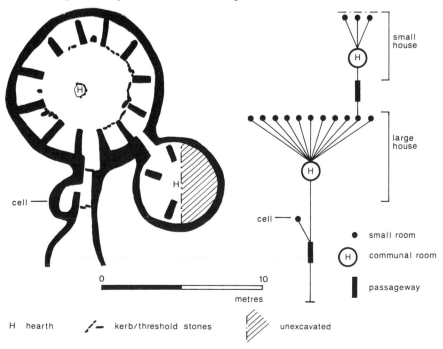

buildings, was controlled. For example, private and secluded areas may be reached only by longer and more tortuous routes. Access analysis can be applied to ancient buildings (figure 39), as well as modern structures, and has been used to considerable effect to interpret the complex changes in settlement layout in Orkney and Caithness during the iron age.

The examination of the different types of round-house that developed in northern Scotland at this time has revealed a remarkable consistency in the basic arrangement of space within these buildings, constructed over a period of seven hundred years. The sizes of these houses can be compared graphically (figure 40). The focus of these dwellings was the hearth, invariably positioned in the middle of a central room. Around this room was a peripheral area, often radially divided, for sleeping and storage. Although the overall dimensions of the ground-floor plans may differ quite considerably, it seems that it was important to these iron age communities that the width of the outer zone did not vary greatly, probably being related to its common use.

Such well-defined arrangements, repeated so consistently over the centuries, reflect the deeply ingrained structure and routine of domestic life. In these circumstances changes in house design tended to occur very gradually. Major transformations will often be linked to external pressures, such as political and economic forces. If strong enough,

40. A graph showing the internal dimensions of northern Scottish iron age round-houses, based on the double-ring plan. The shaded area shows that the width of the peripheral zone in the majority of the houses lies between 1.6 and 2.1 metres. (After Reid, revised.)

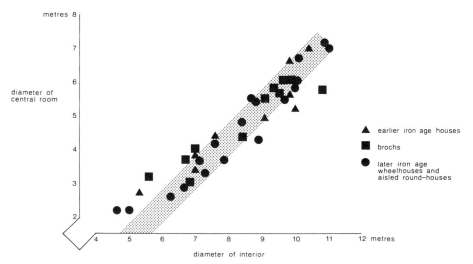

these forces can have a profound effect on social relations and how they are represented by domestic architecture. In Britain, one of the most obvious and widespread examples of such pressure occurred at the end of the iron age. At this time there was a dramatic and sudden change to many aspects of domestic life, including the design of houses. These changes followed the increasing involvement with the Roman world during the first century BC and after the Roman invasion in AD 43.

9
Select gazetteer of places to visit

SCOTLAND

All settlements, with the exception of Scord of Brouster, Shetland, are in the care of Historic Scotland.

BORDERS REGION
Edin's Hall (NT 772603). 3 km south of Stow.

The remains of a broch set within an earlier hillfort. The foundations of other later prehistoric round-houses can also be seen.

HIGHLAND REGION
Carn Liath (NC 870013). 4 km north of Golspie.

The remains of a broch with other buildings, some of which may be contemporary with the broch, surrounded by a defensive wall.

Dun Beag (NG 339386). On the island of Skye, 1 km west of Bracadale.

The remains of a broch, neatly built with squared stones, characteristic of the brochs of Skye.

Dun Dornaigil (NC 457450). 2 km north-east of Eriboll.

Part of the exterior of this broch stands nearly 7 metres high.

Dun Telve (NG 829172). 2.5 km south-east of Glenelg.

The remains of this broch stand to a height of 10 metres.

Dun Troddan (NG 834172). 3 km south-east of Glenelg.

This well-preserved broch is very similar in design to the broch at Dun Telve, 500 metres away.

ORKNEY
Gurness (HY 382268). On the mainland of Orkney, 2 km north-east of Evie.

An extensive and well-preserved iron age settlement, surrounded by defences, with a broch at its centre.

Knap of Howar (HY 483519). On the island of Papa Westray.

An early neolithic farmstead, probably the oldest standing houses in north-west Europe.

Midhowe (HY 372306). On the island of Rousay.
A well-preserved defended broch settlement similar in many respects to Gurness.

Skara Brae (HY 231187). On the mainland of Orkney, 11 km north of Stromness.
The best-preserved group of neolithic stone-built houses to survive in western Europe.

SHETLAND
Clickhimin (HU 464408). On the mainland of Shetland, on the outskirts of Lerwick.
The remains of bronze and iron age farmsteads and a later broch, which dominates a defended enclosure.

Jarlshof (HU 398095). On the mainland of Shetland, 1 km south-east of Sumburgh Airport.
Extensive remains of bronze and iron age settlements, with a range of different house types preserved. One of the wheelhouses stands nearly 3 metres high and is still partially roofed.

Mousa (HU 458237). On the island of Mousa.
The best-preserved of all the broch towers, standing 13 metres high.

Scord of Brouster (HU 256517). On the mainland of Shetland, 3.5 km north-east of Walls.
A settlement of late neolithic and early bronze age date consisting of houses and funerary monuments set within a contemporary field system. Information on the site prepared by the Shetland Amenity Trust.

Stanydale (HU 285502). On the mainland of Shetland, 7 km east of Walls.
A settlement of late neolithic/early bronze age date similar to that at Scord of Brouster. At the centre of this settlement is a large building known as the Temple.

TAYSIDE
Ardestie (NO 502344). 10 km north-east of Dundee.
An iron age settlement dating to the first and second centuries AD and consisting of small stone-built houses and a souterrain.

Carlungie (NO 511359). 13 km north-east of Dundee.
Houses and a souterrain of a similar type to those at the contemporary settlement at Ardestie.

McManus Galleries, Albert Square, Dundee DD1 1DA. Telephone: 0382 23141. City of Dundee District Council.
The archaeology gallery contains a partial lifesize reconstruction of an early iron age post-built ring-ditch house, based on the excavation carried out at Douglasmuir, Tayside.

WESTERN ISLES
Dun Carloway (NB 190412). On the island of Lewis, 2 km south-west of Carloway.
An impressive and well-preserved broch.

WALES

DYFED
Castell Henllys (SN 117391). 7 km east of Newport.
Defended hilltop iron age settlement and Roman period native farmstead. The archaeological excavation of this site has been followed by the reconstruction of buildings on their original sites. Managed by Pembrokeshire Coast National Park (Dyfed County Council).

GWYNEDD
Din Lligwy (SH 496862). On Anglesey, 4 km north of Benllech.
The remains of an enclosed native homestead consisting of round-houses and rectangular buildings, occupied during the fourth century AD. In the care of Cadw (Welsh Historic Monuments).

Ty Mawr, Holyhead Mountain (SH 212820). On Holy Island, Anglesey, 3 km west of Holyhead.
An unenclosed settlement of groups of stone-built round-houses. Most probably constructed in the iron age, but some were occupied during the Roman period. In the care of Cadw (Welsh Historic Monuments).

SOUTH GLAMORGAN
Welsh Folk Museum, St Fagans, Cardiff CF5 6XB. Telephone: 0222 569441. Part of the National Museum of Wales.
A 'Celtic village', with reconstructed buildings based on archaeological evidence from excavated sites throughout Wales. Reproduction furnishings and household implements are used to help illustrate the lives of the inhabitants

ENGLAND

CAMBRIDGESHIRE
Flag Fen Excavations, Forth Drove, Peterborough PE1 5UR. Telephone: 0733 313414.

Major long-term archaeological excavations of this impressive late bronze age waterlogged island site can be seen, together with reconstructions of bronze age and iron age houses. Flag Fen excavations and visitor centre managed by the Fenland Archaeological Trust.

CORNWALL
Carn Euny (SW 402289). 7 km west of Penzance.

The remains of a native farmstead of the Roman period consisting of courtyard houses, overlying an earlier iron age settlement dating back to 500 BC. In the care of English Heritage.

Chysauster (SW 473350). 6 km north of Penzance.

The well-preserved remains of a courtyard-house settlement, occupied during the second and third centuries AD. In the care of English Heritage.

DEVON
Grimspound (SX 701809). 9 km south-west of Moretonhampstead.

A bronze age settlement consisting of 24 stone-built round-houses surrounded by a wide contemporary stone wall. In the care of English Heritage.

Merrivale (SX 553746). 7 km east of Tavistock.

The remains of stone-built bronze age round-houses, associated with funerary and ceremonial monuments and property/field boundaries dating to the same period. In the care of English Heritage.

HAMPSHIRE
Butser Archaeological Farm (SU 723163). 1 km west of Chalton.

A recreation of various aspects of iron age life, including the reconstruction of iron age houses from England and Wales.

ISLES OF SCILLY
Halangy Down (SV 911124). On the island of St Mary's, 2 km north of Hugh Town.

An iron age and Roman period settlement. One of the latest stone-built houses to be constructed on the site was of the courtyard type. In the care of English Heritage.

10
Further reading

Books or articles written for non-specialist readers are indicated by *.

Allen, T., Miles, D., and Palmer, S. 'Iron Age Buildings in the Upper Thames Region' in B. Cunliffe and D. Miles (editors), *Aspects of the Iron Age in Central Southern Britain.* University of Oxford: Committee for Archaeology, Monograph 2, 1984, 89-101.

Armit, I. 'Broch Building in Northern Scotland: The Context of Innovation', *World Archaeology*, 21, 3 (1990), 435-45.

Avery, M., and Close-Brooks, J. 'Shearplace Hill, Sydling St Nicholas, Dorset, House A: A Suggested Re-interpretation', *Proceedings of the Prehistoric Society*, 35 (1969), 345-51.

Barrett, J. C. 'Aspects of the Iron Age in Atlantic Scotland. A Case Study in the Problems of Archaeological Interpretation', *Proceedings of the Society of Antiquaries of Scotland*, 111 (1981), 205-19.

Bradley, R. *The Social Foundations of Prehistoric Britain: Themes and Variations in the Archaeology of Power.* Longman, 1984.

Christie, P. M. 'Cornwall in the Bronze Age', *Cornish Archaeology*, 25 (1986), 81-110.

Clarke, D. V., and Sharples, N. 'Settlements and Subsistence in the Third Millennium BC' in C. Renfrew (editor), *The Prehistory of Orkney, BC 4000-1000 AD.* Edinburgh University Press, 1990, 54-82.

Coles, B., and Coles, J. *Sweet Track to Glastonbury.* Thames & Hudson, 1986.*

Cunliffe, B. *English Heritage Book of Danebury.* Batsford, 1993.*

Cunliffe, B. *Iron Age Communities in Britain.* Routledge, third edition 1991.

Darvill, T. *Prehistoric Britain.* Batsford, 1987.*

Ellison, A. 'Towards a Socioeconomic Model for the Middle Bronze Age in Southern England' in I. Hodder, G. Isaac and N. Hammond (editors), *Pattern of the Past.* Cambridge University Press, 1981, 413-38.

Evans, C. 'Archaeology and Modern Times: Bersu's Woodbury 1938 and 1939', *Antiquity*, 63, 240 (1989), 436-50.

Fleming, A. *The Dartmoor Reaves*. Batsford, 1988.*

Foster, S. 'Analysis of Spatial Patterns in Buildings (Access Analysis) as an Insight into Social Structure: Examples from the Scottish Atlantic Iron Age', *Antiquity*, 63, 238 (1989), 40-50.

Foster, S. 'Transformation in Social Space: The Iron Age of Orkney and Caithness', *Scottish Archaeological Review*, 6 (1989), 34-55.

Guilbert, G. C. 'Double-ring Roundhouses, Probable and Possible, in Prehistoric Britain', *Proceedings of the Prehistoric Society*, 47 (1981), 299-317.

Harding, D. W. 'The Function and Classification of Brochs and Duns' in R. Miket and C. Burgess (editors), *Between and Beyond the Walls*. John Donald, 1984, 206-20.

Hedges, J. W. 'The Broch Period' in C. Renfrew (editor), *The Prehistory of Orkney, BC 4000-1000 AD*. Edinburgh University Press, 1990, 150-75.

Hingley, R. *Rural Settlement in Roman Britain*. Seaby, 1989.

Hingley, R. 'Domestic Organisation and Gender Relations in Iron Age and Romano-British Households' in R. Samson (editor), *The Social Archaeology of Houses*. Edinburgh University Press, 1990, 125-47.

Macinnes, L. 'Brochs and the Roman Occupation of Lowland Scotland', *Proceedings of the Society of Antiquaries of Scotland*, 114 (1984), 235-49.

Megaw, J. V. S., and Simpson, D. D. A. *Introduction to British Prehistory*. Leicester University Press, 1979.

Morrison, I. *Landscape with Lake Dwellings: The Crannogs of Scotland*. Edinburgh University Press, 1985.

Musson, C. 'House-plans and Prehistory', *Current Archaeology*, 21 (1970), 267-75.*

Oliver, P. *Dwellings: The House across the World*. Phaidon, 1987.

Parker Pearson, M. 'Food, Fertility and Front Doors in the First Millennium BC', in T. Champion and J. Collis (editors), *The British Iron Age: Recent Trends*. Collis Publications, forthcoming.

Quinnell, H. 'Cornwall during the Iron Age and Roman Period', *Cornish*

Archaeology, 25 (1986), 111-34.

Reid, M. L. 'A Room with a View: An Examination of Round-houses, with Particular Reference to Northern Britain', *Oxford Journal of Archaeology*, 8, 1 (1989), 1-39.

Reynolds, P. J. *Iron-Age Farm: The Butser Experiment.* Colonnade, 1979.*

Richards, C. 'The Late Neolithic House in Orkney' in R. Samson (editor), *The Social Archaeology of Houses.* Edinburgh University Press, 1990, 111-24.

Richards, C. 'Skara Brae: Revisiting a Neolithic Village in Orkney' in W. S. Hanson and E. A. Slater (editors), *Scottish Archaeology: New Perceptions.* Aberdeen University Press, 1991, 24-43.

Ritchie, A. *Scotland BC.* HMSO, 1988.*

Ritchie, G. and A. *Scotland: Archaeology and Early History.* Edinburgh University Press, second edition 1991.*

Ritchie, J. N. G. *Brochs of Scotland.* Shire, 1988.*

Index

Page numbers in italic refer to illustrations